Saving Electricity

We expect electricity to *be* there at the flick of a switch! But the day will come soon, many experts believe, when we may not have all the electricity we want. This book asks us to take a look at the ways we use—and misuse—electric power today.

The authors tell the story of a power blackout in a small city to explain how the energy of coal, oil, natural gas, nuclear fission, and falling water is used to produce electricity. They explain some of the problems posed by the use of these energy sources. They also describe energy sources we may use in the future.

Finally, the authors explain why it is important to save electricity now. They have a number of suggestions for doing this—all the way from turning off unneeded lights to recycling waste packaging. Young readers will surely have their own suggestions to add to the list.

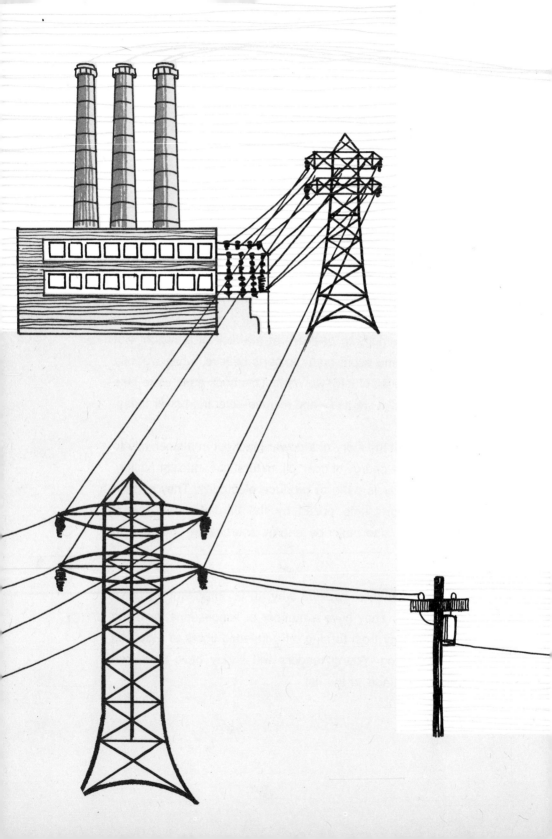

SAVING
ELECTRICITY

By Sam and Beryl Epstein

Pictures by Jeanne Bendick

GARRARD PUBLISHING COMPANY
CHAMPAIGN, ILLINOIS

Acknowledgment

The authors' special thanks
go to James I. Monsell,
Superintendent of Public Utilities,
Village of Greenport, New York,
and Albert Salmon,
Head of Buildings and Grounds,
Southold, New York, Public Schools.

Library of Congress Cataloging in Publication Data

Epstein, Samuel, 1909-
    Saving electricity.

    Includes index.
    SUMMARY: A simple explanation of how electricity
is generated and how it can be conserved.
    1. Electric power production—Juvenile
literature. 2. Electric power—Conservation—
Juvenile literature. [1. Electric power production.
2. Electric power—Conservation] I. Epstein,
Beryl Williams, 1910-   joint author.
II. Bendick, Jeanne. III. Title.
TK1005.E67   621.312   76-46986
ISBN 0-8116-6107-5

Contents

1. Blackout

At seven-thirty one dark winter morning, Jimmy Morris stood in front of the open refrigerator. He was trying to decide what kind of jelly he wanted on his toast.

Suddenly the refrigerator light went out. So did the kitchen light. The electric coffee maker gurgled several times and stopped.

Mr. Morris had left the TV on when he went to work. Now it was silent.

"Oh, dear!" Mrs. Morris said. "The fuse must have blown."

Jimmy looked out the window. "All of the houses are dark! Maybe my battery radio will tell us what is happening."

While his mother lighted a candle, Jimmy turned on his radio.

The announcer was reading the news. "Riverton is having a blackout," he said. "The Riverton Electric Company still does not know how long it will last."

"Maybe there won't be any school today!" Jimmy said.

"And I suppose I won't be working at the dress shop," Mrs. Morris said.

The announcer was still talking. He was naming places that could supply their own electric power in an

emergency. One was the radio station. Others were the Riverton Hospital and the Northside School.

That was Jimmy's school. So he finished breakfast and went out to meet his classmate Judy.

They walked to school together along the dark streets. All the traffic lights were out.

At the gas station Mr. Wheeler was putting up a sign. It said:

SORRY!
WE CAN'T PUMP GAS
WITHOUT ELECTRICITY

Lights were shining through the school windows, but they were not as bright as usual. Inside, Judy saw that only half of the ceiling light tubes in the hall were on. The other half had been removed. In their classroom only the lights away from the windows were on.

Just as Mrs. Brown was saying good morning to the class, Mr. Stevens, the principal, started to talk over the loudspeaker.

"We make our own electricity," he

said, "but we can't make as much as we normally need. So there will be changes in our program today. Neither the gym nor the auditorium will be used. There will be no sewing or cooking classes, and no shop classes in woodworking or metalworking."

When the principal finished, everyone in Mrs. Brown's class wanted to talk about the blackout.

Mrs. Brown did too. She said, "We all use electricity every day. We ought to know something about it. And we should find out why Riverton has lost its electric power."

Mrs. Brown had asked an expert to talk to the class later in the morning. This was Mr. Plaski, who was in charge of all the school's machinery.

"Mr. Plaski is very busy today," Mrs.

Brown said. "But he will show us the machine that is making electricity. It is called a generator."

Then she explained two words Mr. Plaski might use: *watt* and *kilowatt*.

"We measure electric power by watts," she said. "That is why you see that word, or the letter *W*, on light bulbs. A bulb marked 100-watt gives us a bright light. A bulb marked 75-watt gives less light because it draws less electricity. A kilowatt is 1,000 watts."

I KILOWATT = 1,000 WATTS

2. A Lesson in the Basement

At ten o'clock Mrs. Brown led the class to the basement. Two other classes were already there, and Mr. Plaski was waiting for them beside a closed door.

"We call this our generating room because the machine inside it is our generating plant," he said. He opened the door.

In the room was a large rounded metal case, or cylinder. It looked

something like a metal garbage can lying on its side. At one end was an engine, which was roaring loudly.

Mr. Plaski shut the door so he wouldn't have to shout.

"The round case is our electric generator," he said. "The engine that runs it is like the engine of a truck. Together they are called a generating plant."

Mr. Plaski said he would explain how a generator makes electricity. But first he asked if the students knew anything about magnets.

"We did some magnet experiments in class," a girl said. "We saw how a magnet can pick up tacks and iron filings."

"We did something else with a magnet," Mrs. Brown reminded her

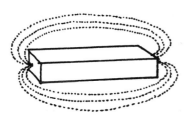
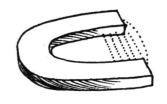

MAGNETIC FIELD,
BAR MAGNET

MAGNETIC FIELD,
HORSESHOE MAGNET

class. "First we sprinkled some iron filings on a piece of paper. Then we held a bar magnet under the paper. What happened?"

"When we jiggled the paper a little, the filings moved," Jimmy said. "They formed curved lines that reached from one end of the magnet to the other. They showed us the magnet's invisible power."

Mr. Plaski nodded. "The area where those lines are is called a magnetic

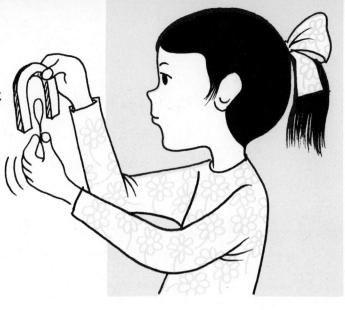

MOVING THE WIRE LOOP IN AND OUT OF THE MAGNETIC FIELD GENERATES ELECTRICITY

field, and there is something quite interesting about it. Suppose you slip a loop of wire over the magnet so that the wire is in the magnetic field. If you just let the wire stay there, nothing happens. But if you move it in and out of the magnetic field, electricity will be produced. That is, electricity will be generated in the wire."

"Why does moving the loop make electricity?" a girl asked.

17

"No one really knows," Mr. Plaski said. "We only know that it does. Of course, one small magnet and one loop of wire can produce very little electricity. But there are powerful magnets inside the metal case of the school generator. They form a sort of tunnel. A rod called the generator shaft extends through this tunnel. Fastened to this shaft are many loops, or coils, of wire. When the shaft is spun around, those loops pass in and out of the powerful magnetic fields. And this generates a lot of electricity."

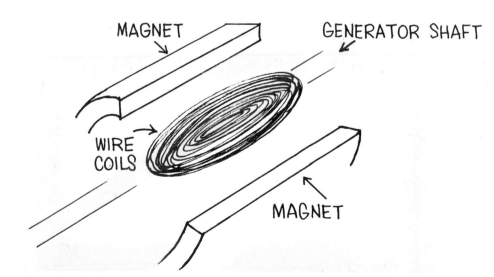

Mr. Plaski explained that the generator shaft was turned by the engine. "Our engine runs on gasoline," he continued. "But the huge generators at the Riverton Electric Company are turned by turbines. Turbines are engines that run on steam. The steam comes from boilers heated by burning fuel oil."

Then Mr. Plaski explained that the school's emergency generator could produce 65 kilowatts of electric power. "Now I'll show you what we're doing with those 65 kilowatts," he said.

He led the students down a flight of stairs and into a room with two roaring furnaces.

"These furnaces heat water that heats the school," Mr. Plaski said. "They use fuel oil, but they can't work without electric motors. The motors do three things. Some run pumps that force oil into the furnaces. Others run blowers that force air into the furnaces so the oil will burn. The rest force the heated water through radiators in every room of the school. Our heating system uses about 10 of our 65 kilowatts. Now let's see where the other 55 kilowatts go."

Upstairs Mr. Plaski showed them that he had removed half of the ceiling lights in the halls. "This saves half the electricity we usually use in the halls," he said. "Even so, we are using about 10 more of our kilowatts. So we have 45 left."

At the cafeteria he pointed out some of the things that use electric power there: refrigerators, freezers, dishwashers, ovens, food warmers, fans that carry away cooking odors, and many lights.

"This cafeteria uses another 20 kilowatts," he explained.

"So now there are only 25 left," Judy said.

Mr. Plaski nodded. "And we need them all to supply some lights in our classrooms and offices. So you see why there are no cooking or sewing or shop classes today. We can't send power to the electrical equipment in those rooms. The auditorium and gym can't be used because we don't have the power for their many bright lights."

"But suppose that you did turn on the gym lights today," Jimmy asked. "Would the generator blow up?"

"No," Mr. Plaski said. "But I would

be asking the generator to do more work than it is able to do. A special control would shut it off immediately. The school would have no more power. We would have our own blackout."

"Is that what happened to the electric company today?" Judy asked.

"Exactly," Mr. Plaski said. "But so many things happened before that. Suppose I tell you the whole story from the beginning."

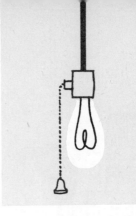

3. Electricity for Riverton

Like many other towns, Riverton got its first electric generating plant around 1900, Mr. Plaski told the students. The new Riverton Electric Company also put up the poles and the wires that carried electric power all over town.

At first people used the electricity mostly for lighting. Most electrical appliances had not been invented.

Then new electrical items, such as fans and vacuum cleaners, began to

appear. Electric motors to run machinery were invented. The town put up electric street lights.

After several years, people were using all the power the electric company could supply. So the company bought a second generator.

To sell as much electricity as possible, the company advertised. Its ads said: "Electric Power Is Cheap. It Is Clean and Convenient. Use More."

As the years went by, people began using electricity in many ways. They kept food cold and fresh in electric refrigerators. They washed clothes in electric washers and ironed them with electric irons.

They bought electric water heaters and electric stoves, freezers, radios, and record players. They heated buildings with electricity.

Meanwhile, the city of Riverton was growing. New factories were springing up. They used still more electricity.

The electric company bought two more generators. It was still urging people to use more electricity. And people did use more. They bought air conditioners and television sets. They bought electric blankets, toothbrushes, razors, clothes dryers and hair dryers, carving knives, corn poppers, and dozens of other things.

"The engineers who control the Riverton Electric Company's four huge generators keep a sharp eye on the clock these days," Mr. Plaski said.

"Why do they do that?" a girl asked.

"Because people seem to use differ-ent amounts of electricity at different times of the day," Mr. Plaski told her. "The times when lots of electricity is being used are called peak-load periods. The times when less electricity is being used are called off-peak periods.

"At about ten o'clock at night, for example," he went on, "an off-peak

period starts. Many people turn off lights and TV's because they are going to bed. So about ten o'clock the engineers shut down one or two of the generators. They leave these shut down until five or six in the morning. That's the beginning of one peak-load period, because people are getting up. Another peak-load period starts in late afternoon."

Then he explained that the Riverton company could usually supply enough electricity for peak-load periods by using only three of its four generators.

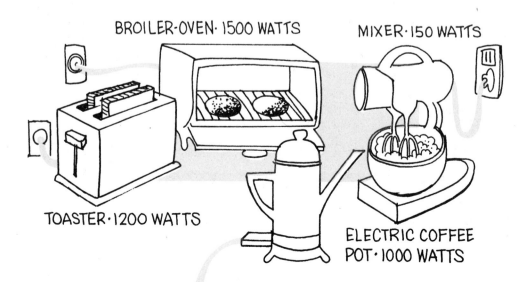

BROILER-OVEN· 1500 WATTS

MIXER· 150 WATTS

TOASTER· 1200 WATTS

ELECTRIC COFFEE POT· 1000 WATTS

"But if the weather is hot or very cold, many air conditioners or heaters may be turned on," Mr. Plaski said. "That can bring about an extra-heavy peak load. So the engineers watch thermometers and weather forecasts too. When they expect an extra-heavy peak load, they make sure all four generators are running."

He said that the engineers could also get extra power from outside Riverton if they needed it. They could get it over the power lines that link together a network of generating

HOT PLATE·UP TO 1650 WATTS

COLOR TV·420 WATTS

STEW POT·1320 WATTS

BLOW DRYER· 1000 WATTS

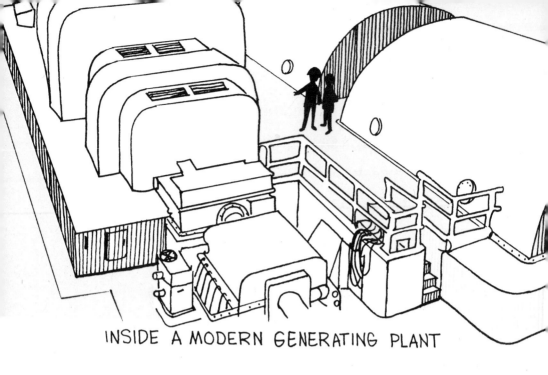

INSIDE A MODERN GENERATING PLANT

plants. The network is called a grid, and it links together all the plants in several states.

Sometimes, Mr. Plaski explained, Riverton sent power to the grid. It did that when there was a need elsewhere and the Riverton plant had power to share.

"But this morning," Mr. Plaski said, "the Riverton plant needed extra power. One of its generators had been shut down for servicing. The engineers expected an extra-heavy peak load, because the weather had turned so cold here in the valley. A message went out to the grid, and by six o'clock extra power was flowing into Riverton's lines. Riverton had all the electricity it needed."

"Then why did we have a blackout?" Judy asked.

AT THE CONTROL PANEL

"Because a truck skidded off an icy road and crashed into one of the steel towers carrying the grid's power lines," Mr. Plaski said. "The lines tore loose, and power from the grid was cut off. Riverton's three working generators were suddenly asked to do more than they can do. Their safety controls went into action, and they stopped producing electricity."

"How long will the blackout last?" Jimmy asked.

"It may be ended already in one part of Riverton. But it probably won't be completely over until tonight," Mr. Plaski said.

The students were puzzled by his answer. He explained it.

"Let's use refrigerators as examples," he said. "They run until the food inside is cold enough. Then they shut off for a while. All the refrigerators in Riverton are not running every minute of the day.

"But when the blackout happened," he went on, "all the refrigerators in town stopped running. By now the air inside all of them is warming up. If the power came back on all over Riverton, every refrigerator in town would start running immediately. So would water heaters, furnaces, and other electrical equipment. The town would be trying to use more power than it uses even in a peak-load period. The electric company's generators would be asked to do more than they can do."

Jimmy spoke up. "Then the safety controls on the generators would shut them off," he said. "There would be another blackout."

"Exactly!" Mr. Plaski said. "But if power is sent to only one part of Riverton at a time, the generators can handle the extra-heavy load. And that extra-heavy load won't last very long. Refrigerators will stop running after they cool off inside. Furnaces will shut off when buildings warm up. Then the electric company will be able to send power to another part of town too."

Mr. Plaski reminded them of one more thing. "The Riverton Electric Company still needs extra power from the grid today because of the cold weather. We can't get extra power until the lines are repaired, and that may take all day. That's why the blackout may not be completely over until tonight."

4. Why Not More Generating Plants?

Back in the classroom Jimmy had a question: "Why doesn't the electric company buy more generators so we can have all the power we want?"

Mrs. Brown told him it was difficult for the company to find suitable places to put more generators. "Most people in Riverton don't want new electric plants near their homes," she said. "Everybody is afraid a new plant will pollute the air with smoke from its burning fuels."

1. FUEL COMES IN.
2. IT MAKES STEAM IN A HUGE BOILER
3. WHICH DRIVES A TURBINE
4. WHICH TURNS A GENERATOR, TO MAKE
   ELECTRICITY.
5. ELECTRICITY IS SENT THROUGH WIRES,
   ON ITS WAY TO YOUR HOUSE.

Jimmy and the other students had already learned about air pollution. They knew dirty air can make people sick and can harm other living things.

Mrs. Brown explained that most generating plants burn some kind of fuel. The fuel's heat turns the water into steam. The steam runs the machines that make electricity. One kind of fuel is natural gas. It is called a clean fuel because it does not pollute the air very much. Certain grades of oil are also clean fuels. Other grades of oil are dirty fuels. They cause a lot of air pollution. Soft coal is also a dirty fuel.

"Riverton's plant now burns a clean grade of oil that causes very little pollution," Mrs. Brown said. "So people have not minded living near it. But the world is rapidly using up its supply of clean fuel. All plants may have to burn dirty fuel in the future. That's why people don't want generating plants near their homes."

Mrs. Brown said scientists are trying to find ways to clean up the dirty fuels, or to burn them without polluting the air. The only ways found so far are expensive.

Jimmy thought of a new question: "Isn't there a way to make electricity without burning fuel?"

Mrs. Brown said there were several ways. Using atomic power is one way. To explain, she told the class something about atoms.

Everything in the world is made up of atoms, which are so tiny they can't be seen. There are many kinds of atoms. A few kinds can be split, and when they split they give off heat.

If a great many of these atoms split at one time, they give off so much heat that there is an explosion. That is what happens when an atomic bomb is set off.

"But it is possible to control the rate of splitting," Mrs. Brown said. "Then the atoms give off heat without causing an explosion. That heat can be used to make steam for generating plants."

1. AN ATOMIC PARTICLE LANDS IN THE NUCLEUS OF AN ATOM

2. MAKING IT SPLIT.

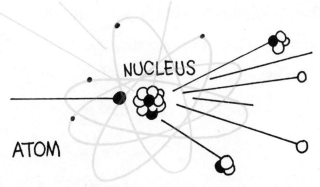

NUCLEUS

ATOM

3. WHEN A NUCLEUS SPLITS, IT GIVES OFF HEAT.

Some atomic generating plants have already been built. More are being planned. Some people say that atomic plants will save oil and gas for the future. And they say these plants don't pollute the air.

"But other people are worried about atomic plants," Mrs. Brown said. "They think that we don't yet know how to use atomic energy safely. The atomic materials give off rays that are deadly to all living things. These rays could escape from an atomic plant through an accident or through an explosion. No one can promise that this will never happen. There is also a problem with the leftover material, called atomic waste. This too is deadly, and no one knows how to get rid of it safely."

Then Mrs. Brown talked about other ways of generating electricity without burning fuel.

The water of a river can be used to produce electricity. First the river must be dammed to make a big lake. Then a generating plant is built at the foot of the dam. Water from the lake rushes down a big pipe to the plant. It spins a kind of water wheel, which runs the generator that produces electricity.

But not every river can be dammed to make a big lake. Some are too small.

"And each time we dam up a river," Mrs. Brown pointed out, "a lot of land is flooded by the lake. Many people feel we can't afford to lose more land this way."

IN THE FUTURE, WE WILL GET POWER TO
MAKE ELECTRICITY IN MANY WAYS:

FROM THE SUN

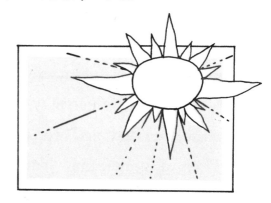

FROM THE WIND

FROM HOT SPRINGS, FED
BY THE EARTH'S HEAT

FROM THE OCEAN

Then Mrs. Brown talked about other kinds of power that can be used to produce electricity. None of these is dangerous. None floods valuable land. None uses up precious natural resources such as clean fuels.

The power of the wind, for example, can turn windmills which can run generators. Generators can also be run by the power of the ocean's tides and waves. And electricity can be produced by the light and the heat of the sun.

"There is just one thing wrong with all these methods," Mrs. Brown said. "At present they cannot produce large amounts of electric power. Perhaps someday they will. But that may take many years."

Jimmy suddenly had an idea. "Why

don't we all start saving as much electricity as we can?" he said. "Maybe if we save enough, we won't need to build more generating plants for a long time. And maybe, by then, somebody will discover ways of making lots of electricity—ways that won't need more dams and that won't be dangerous and won't pollute the air."

"That's a fine idea," Mrs. Brown said. "Saving electricity is an important job for all of us."

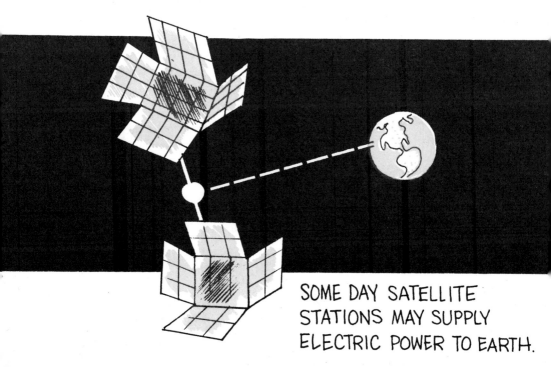

SOME DAY SATELLITE STATIONS MAY SUPPLY ELECTRIC POWER TO EARTH.

5. Saving Electricity

"Many people are looking for ways to use less electricity," Mrs. Brown said.

Mr. Plaski wanted to save electricity in the school. He thought half of the hall lights were enough to light the halls safely. The students agreed.

"Here's another of his ideas," Mrs. Brown said. She pointed to the long metal cabinet under the windows. The students knew it covered the radiator. She told them it also covered an electric fan that brought in fresh air from outside. Each classroom had its fresh-air fan.

"None of them is running today," Mrs. Brown said. "So I opened two of our windows at the top. Mr. Plaski thinks all the classrooms can get fresh air that way from now on, unless the weather is very windy or rainy. Don't you think he's right?"

Everyone nodded.

Mrs. Brown told the class to look

OPEN THE WINDOWS AT THE TOP FOR FRESH AIR

up at the lights. They were the same kind of long white tubes that lighted the halls. They are called fluorescent lights, and they are different from ordinary light bulbs.

Inside an ordinary bulb is a wire called a filament. It glows white hot when electricity passes through it. The bulb's light comes from the glowing filament.

A fluorescent tube has no filament. Instead the inside of the tube has been coated with a chemical. When electricity passes through the tube, the chemical glows brightly and gives off light.

"Each of our fluorescent tubes uses only 40 watts," Mrs. Brown said. "But each one gives more light than a 100-watt bulb, so it saves electricity.

These lights also cut down on the school's electric bill."

"We have two fluorescent lights at home," Judy said. "Ours are circles. One is in the kitchen, and one is in the bathroom."

Mrs. Brown then told them about other ways of saving electricity. There is a new kind of refrigerator that has especially thick walls to keep warm air out. Its motor doesn't have to run so often to keep the inside of the refrigerator cool. "This kind is more expensive to buy than an ordinary refrigerator," Mrs. Brown said. "But in several years it saves enough electricity to pay for the extra cost."

Then she talked about electric clothes washers, dishwashers, and kitchen ranges.

"It takes nearly as much electricity to run washing machines with part loads as it does to run them with full loads," she said. "So it saves electricity to wash one full load of clothes instead of several smaller loads. The same is true for dishwashers. It also saves electricity to bake or roast a few things at a time in an electric oven."

Mrs. Brown went on. "I used to keep my house very warm in cold weather. Now I keep it several degrees cooler, and the electric motors in the furnace don't have to run so often. If I get cold, I put on a sweater. I have also stopped using my air conditioner as often as I used to. I save a lot of electric power by turning it on only when the weather is very hot."

Next Mrs. Brown explained how recycling paper, cans, and bottles can save electricity.

KEEP WARM WITH A SWEATER

KEEP COOL WITHOUT THE AIR CONDITIONER

"Let's take paper first," she said. "Most of it is made from wood pulp. Turning pulp into paper takes a lot of electricity. It does not take as much electricity to make new paper out of old paper."

Making new cans out of old tin and aluminum cans also saves a lot of electric power.

"Huge amounts of electricity are needed to make aluminum," Mrs.

Brown said. "We really should stop using aluminum cans, if we want to save electricity."

Then she talked about bottles. The class knew that old bottles can be ground up and used to make new bottles, bricks, or other things.

"But the best thing to do with glass bottles is to use returnable ones," Mrs. Brown said. "These bottles can be washed and used over and over again. Cleaning a bottle uses only one-third as much electricity as it takes to make a new one."

Another way to use less electricity is not to waste it, Mrs. Brown pointed out. She asked the students to think of ways electricity was wasted in their homes.

Everyone agreed that leaving lights and TVs on in empty rooms wastes electricity.

"What about keeping the refrigerator door open while you decide what you want?" Mrs. Brown asked. "How many of you do that?"

Almost everyone raised a hand.

"An open door lets warm air get inside," Mrs. Brown said. "Then the motor runs to cool the refrigerator again. Putting warm food into a refrigerator wastes electricity too. Let the food cool before you put it in."

She spoke about wasting water. "Do

you run water when you don't need it?" she asked. "Do you sometimes leave faucets dripping?"

"How can wasting water waste electricity?" a boy asked.

"Water is forced into the pipes in your house by electric pumps," Mrs. Brown explained. "The more water you run, the longer the pumps work. The longer they work, the more electricity they use.

"In many homes water is heated by electricity," she went on. "Wasting hot water in those homes wastes even more electric power—the power it took to heat the water."

"Does heating water use a lot of electricity?" Judy asked.

Mrs. Brown took a little book from her desk drawer. "This booklet from

AN ELECTRIC COMPANY SELLS POWER BY THE KILOWATT HOUR—ONE KILOWATT OF ELECTRICITY USED FOR ONE HOUR. AN ELECTRIC METER RECORDS THE KILOWATT HOURS A CUSTOMER USES.

the Riverton Electric Company should tell us," she said. "Yes, here it is. It takes about one-quarter of a kilowatt-hour to heat one gallon of water."

"Here are some other interesting facts," she said. "A dripping faucet can waste about three gallons of water a day. If that is hot water, three-quarters of a kilowatt-hour of electricity is being wasted. And a tub bath usually takes about twice as much water as a shower. So showering instead of bathing saves electricity too."

Mrs. Brown closed the little book. "And now let's talk about peak-load periods," she said. "You remember that Mr. Plaski told us that the Riverton Electric Company uses all four of its generators only during heavy peak-load periods. At other times only two or three of its generators are running. So if we used less power during peak-load periods, the company would not have to build a new plant."

She used the school's buses to explain how her suggestion would work.

"Suppose 500 students in our school use buses," she said. "If each bus carries 50 students, we would need ten buses. But if 250 students came to school an hour earlier, and left an hour earlier, five buses could do the job. They could bring those 250 students to school first, and bring the other 250 an hour later. They could take the students home the same way.

"By making five buses do the work of ten," Mrs. Brown went on, "we would be spreading the same work over more hours. We can do that with electric power too. We can spread out our housework, for example, so that more of it is done during off peak-load periods."

Mrs. Brown said that some electric companies are now asking their customers to do just that. Some companies even charge a lower rate for electricity used during off-peak periods. This encourages people to shift some uses of electricity to those hours.

6. A Family Plan

When Jimmy left school that afternoon, he had a list of ways to save electricity. Everyone in the class had helped make the list. Everyone had a copy to take home.

Jimmy's house was just beginning to warm up. The power had been turned on in that part of town only half an hour earlier.

That night at the supper table, Jimmy showed his mother and father the list.

"We already do some of these things," Mrs. Morris said. "We usually turn lights off when we leave a room."

"We usually do," Mr. Morris agreed. "But sometimes we don't. In the past electricity was plentiful and cheap. So we never really put our minds to the job of saving it. Now things are different."

"Some of these ideas are new to me," Mrs. Morris said. "Take this matter of peak loads. I can do something about that. I can manage to wash, dry, and iron clothes in off-peak hours.

"I won't turn the dishwasher on until after nine o'clock tonight," she went on. "And I'll bake the cake for tomorrow's P.T.A. meeting after nine o'clock too."

"It takes no more electricity to bake two cakes than it does to bake one," Jimmy said. "Maybe you could bake us a cake too?"

"Now that's a great way to save electricity!" Mr. Morris said.

The next morning Jimmy's alarm clock went off at seven. He turned on his light and dressed quickly. At the bedroom door he saw the sign he had put there the night before. It said: TURN LIGHTS OUT! He snapped the switch before he left the room.

There was another sign pasted on the mirror in the bathroom. This one said: REMEMBER! DON'T WASTE WATER!

A sign near the bathroom door reminded him to turn off the light.

Jimmy's mother was in the kitchen. His father was in the living room watching the TV news.

Jimmy stood in front of the refrigerator and thought for a moment. There was a sign on the door that said: DON'T DAWDLE! OPEN DOORS WASTE ELECTRICITY! Jimmy decided he wanted peach jam for his toast. He opened the door, took the jam out quickly, and shut the door.

The TV stopped, and Mr. Morris came into the kitchen. He smiled at Jimmy. "I turned it off," he said. Then he said good-bye and left for work.

"Are you going to work today, mom?" Jimmy asked.

"Yes," Mrs. Morris said. "You know, Jimmy, I've been thinking. Mrs. Stokes uses far too many lights in that store. I'm going to suggest that she turn some of them off. That will cut down on the big electric bill she pays every month."

"It'll save electricity too," Jimmy reminded her. "And that's even more important."

DON'T DAWDLE!
OPEN DOORS WASTE
ELECTRICITY!

Index